FERDINAND MAGELLAN

Please visit our web site at: **www.worldalmanaclibrary.com**
For a free color catalog describing World Almanac® Library's list of high-quality books
and multimedia programs, call 1-800-848-2928 (USA) or 1-800-387-3178 (Canada).
World Almanac® Library's fax: (414) 332-3567.

Library of Congress Cataloging-in-Publication Data

Bastable, Tony.
     Ferdinand Magellan / by Tony Bastable.
          p. cm. — (Great explorers)
     Includes bibliographical references and index.
     Summary: Profiles Portuguese explorer Ferdinand Magellan, the first person known to have sailed around the world,
and introduces some of lands, people, plants, and animals he discovered on his journeys
          ISBN 0-8368-5016-5 (lib. bdg.)
          ISBN 0-8368-5176-5 (softcover)
          1. Magalhães, Fernão de, d. 1521—Journeys—Juvenile literature. 2. Explorers—Portugal—Biography—Juvenile
literature. 3. Voyages around the world—Juvenile literature. [1. Magellan, Ferdinand, d. 1521. 2. Explorers.
3. Voyages around the world.] I. Title. II. Great explorers (Milwaukee, Wis.)
     G286.M2B43 2003
     910'.92—dc21
     [B]   2003041189

This North American edition first published in 2004 by
World Almanac® Library
330 West Olive Street, Suite 100
Milwaukee, Wisconsin 53212 USA

This U.S. edition copyright © 2004 by World Almanac® Library.
Created with original © 2003 by Quartz Editions,
112 Station Road, Edgware HA8 7AQ, U.K.
Additional end matter copyright © 2004 by World Almanac® Library.

Series Editor: Tamara Green
World Almanac® Library editor: Alan Wachtel
World Almanac® Library designer: Melissa Valuch

The creators and publishers of this volume wish to thank the following for their kind permission to feature
illustration material: Front cover: main image, Helen Jones/ other images (from top to bottom) AKG/Stuart
Brendon/Tony Stone Images/AKG/Tony Stone Images; Back cover: (from top to bottom) AKG/Bridgeman Art
Library/Tony Stone Images/Bridgeman Art Library/AKG/Bridgeman Art Library; 5 t AKG/c Tony Stone Images/
b Bridgeman Art Library; 6 tl Ancient Art & Architecture Collection/c, b Bridgeman Art Library; 7 Helen Jones;
8 t Bridgeman Art Library/c AKG/b Bridgeman Art Library; 10 t Tony Stone Images/b Bridgeman Art Library;
11 t AKG/c Bridgeman Art Library; 12-13 Stuart Brendon; 14 t, b Bridgeman Art Library; 15 Bridgeman Art
Library; 16 t Bridgeman Art Library/c Tony Stone Images/b AKG; 17 Bridgeman Art Library; 18 t AKG/
b Bridgeman Art Library; 19 t, b AKG; 20 t AKG/b Mary Evans Picture Library; 21 Bridgeman Art Library;
22 AKG; 24 t, c Bridgeman Art Library/b AKG; 25 AKG; 26 t Mary Evans Picture Library/b Ancient Art &
Architecture Collection; 27 t Bridgeman Art Library/b Mary Evans Picture Library; 28 t The Art Archive/
b Mary Evans Picture Library; 30 t, c AKG/b Bridgeman Art Library; 31 Bridgeman Art Library; 32 t, b Tony
Stone Images/c NHPA, V. G. Canseco; b Bridgeman Art Library; 34 t NHPA, H. Palo Jr/b NHPA, G. I. Bernard;
35 t The Art Archive/b AKG; 36 t NHPA, K. Schafer/b Bridgeman Art Library; 38 t Mary Evans Picture Library/
b Bridgeman Art Library; 39 Mary Evans Picture Library; 40 t The Art Archive/c Mary Evans Picture Library/
b AKG; 42 AKG; 43 Helen Jones

Printed in Canada

1 2 3 4 5 6 7 8 9 07 06 05 04 03

GREAT EXPLORERS

FERDINAND
MAGELLAN

TONY BASTABLE

WORLD ALMANAC® LIBRARY

CONTENTS

INTRODUCTION

The *Vittoria* (*above*) was the only one of Magellan's five ships that survived the whole voyage, becoming the first ship to sail around the world.

FERDINAND MAGELLAN achieved his goals through hard work, his own talents, and a refusal to be beaten. His ultimate triumph was one of the greatest sea voyages ever made.

Ferdinand Magellan was already about 25 years old when he first went to sea, and he died at the young age of forty-one. Magellan's active life of seamanship and exploration, therefore, spanned only sixteen years.

Employed by Francisco d'Almeida, the first Portuguese viceroy of India, Magellan learned how to handle a ship and command a crew on the Indian Ocean.

Brightly colored talking parrots were among the many entertaining and curious creatures that were unfamiliar to Magellan.

On Magellan's return to Portugal, however, King Manuel, who did not like him, refused him a position. The adventurer then sought and found another master — Spain — which provided the opportunity for his name to live on. Magellan was to sail the Atlantic, then cross South America through a passage he discovered, and become the first European to cross another mighty ocean, which he named the Pacific. He would not, however, live to see the end of this epic journey.

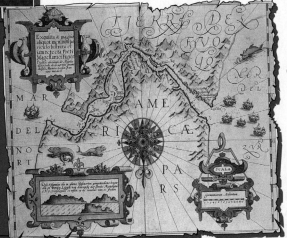

This map, made about 86 years after Magellan's death, shows the famous Strait of Magellan. Magellan's exploration of this narrow sea passage prevented the need to sail around the tip of South America.

Ferdinand Magellan's story is one of determination and courage. Immensely brave and fueled by a driving ambition, he battled on against great challenges.

Prepare to meet a man whose efforts led to the first circumnavigation of the globe.

FERDINAND MAGELLAN

MASTER NAVIGATOR

This painting shows a view of Lisbon, Portugal, the city from which Magellan sailed before he switched allegiance to Portugal's rival, Spain.

Ferdinand Magellan worked hard for everything he achieved. A solid education and a determined nature helped him to overcome many difficulties.

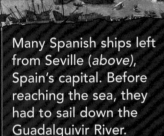

Many Spanish ships left from Seville (*above*), Spain's capital. Before reaching the sea, they had to sail down the Guadalquivir River.

This map of the East Indies shows the islands of Java, Borneo, and many others that Magellan and his crew visited in the course of their circumnavigation of the world. They stopped at these islands in order to trade for local spices.

The late fifteenth century was certainly an exciting age for a young man with a fervent desire for adventure.

Although Ferdinand Magellan's family had noble connections, money was always short. At the age of 12, he was sent to work as a page in a royal court.

This may not sound like the sort of experience to inspire a future seafarer. At the court of Queen Leonor of Portugal, however, Magellan was exposed to more than just music, dancing, and good manners. He also learned jousting, hunting, fencing, swordsmanship, and other skills. Because the Portuguese

> *This must have been a man of courage, valiant in thoughts and undertakings.*
>
> BISHOP LAS CASAS

had a great seafaring tradition, Magellan learned how to make maps and how to find his way when sailing by the stars, too.

In 1488, Bartholomew Diaz, a Portuguese explorer, reached the Cape of Good Hope, the gateway to the Indian Ocean and the route to India and the Spice Islands. Then, in 1493, when Ferdinand was about thirteen years old, Christopher Columbus arrived back in triumph from his voyage to the Caribbean, believing he had discovered a westerly route to the spices and jewels of the Orient. The news spread like wildfire, and King John of Portugal ordered a fleet to be fitted out to sail in search of a similar route westward to India.

Magellan, who was to become one of the greatest seafarers of all time, first learned to navigate at the court of Queen Leonor of Portugal. He also studied astronomy and geography.

Dom Manuel — who some believe was hostile to Magellan — succeeded King John II after the king was assassinated. Manuel is seen in this detail from an anonymous modern painting (*right*).

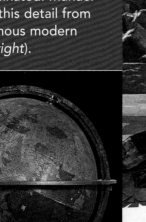

Magellan may have become convinced the world was round when he saw the globe (*above*) in the royal map room. It had been made by German-born cartographer Martin Behaim, mapmaker for the Portuguese throne.

Magellan's highly embellished signature (*below*) is taken from a letter to the Emperor Charles V, sent from Seville and dated October 24, 1518.

At every European port, men competed to join the crews of ships sailing to faraway places.

BLATANT PREJUDICE

Magellan sought similar adventures, but his first slice of bad luck was about to be served. The man who supervised the pages at the Queen's court, Duke Manuel, was the king's brother-in-law. Some people believe the Duke took an instant dislike to young Magellan.

By keeping quiet and working hard, Magellan no doubt thought he would succeed in entering the king's service. The tragedy was that in 1495, King John of Portugal was poisoned, and his successor was Duke Manuel himself.

How envious Magellan might have felt in September 1499 when Vasco da Gama returned from opening up the sea route to India! Da Gama's cargo of spices, jewels, silks, and jade was worth a fortune. Everyone soon wanted a share of such rich rewards. To obtain a berth on a ship sailing to the Orient, however, required considerable influence.

In 1505, at the age of twenty-five, Magellan had his chance. He, his brother, and their cousin were allowed to join the largest Portuguese expeditionary fleet ever to sail. Consisting of twenty-two ships, it was to take control of India and the sea route to it from Portugal.

Magellan started his career at sea not as an officer, but as a supernumerary seaman. This meant he received board and lodging only. Hard work helped him rise to become a sea captain. His prime concern as a captain was to keep Arab traders out of the Indian Ocean so that only Portuguese commercial ships could sail in the region.

> " *May I be permitted to seek service under another lord?*
>
> MAGELLAN TO MANUEL, KING OF PORTUGAL, AFTER HAVING BEEN REFUSED A POSITION "

Later, he was to fight in one of the most extraordinary naval battles ever. Near the island of Diu, off India's Malabar coast, the Portuguese, with just nineteen ships and fewer than two thousand men, overcame an Arab force of twenty thousand. Magellan was seriously wounded.

Other dangers also arose. The Sultan of Melaka, for example, pretended to welcome the Portuguese but was secretly plotting to murder them. Sixty men were killed, but Magellan escaped at the last moment. When the Portuguese finally conquered Melaka in 1511, Magellan was there and took part in the battle.

By 1513, Magellan had become a member of the Portuguese army. During that year, while serving in Morocco, he was wounded again — so badly that he walked with a limp for the rest of his life.

Another important event in Magellan's life also took place in Morocco. The commander of the Portuguese army there believed Magellan had made a business deal with the enemy and reported it to King Manuel. Magellan returned to Portugal in 1514 — more than thirty-five years old, lame, tired, flat broke — and disgraced. The king refused him a new position and released him from the service of Portugal.

Magellan's name is written differently in different languages. In English, of course, it is written as "Ferdinand Magellan." In Spanish, it was written "Hernando de Magallanes." In his native Portuguese, it was written as "Fernao de Magalhaes."

TIME LINE

c. 1480
Magellan is born in Portugal. In 1492, he becomes a page at the court of Queen Leonor.

1505-1513
Magellan travels to India, eastern Africa, Malaysia, and Morocco. He takes part in the conquest of Melaka. He is wounded during a campaign to suppress Moorish rebels in Morocco. He transfers his services to Spain's King Charles I of Castile.

1519-20
Magellan sails west and discovers the strait that now bears his name. Three of his five ships become the first European vessels to enter the Pacific Ocean.

1521
Food supplies run out. Ships land on Pukapuka Island. Magellan arrives in Guam. He dies on April 27 in a battle on the beach of Mactan Island in the Philippines. Survivors burn the *Concepción.* Two ships, the *Vittoria* and the *Trinidad,* reach the Moluccas and take valuable cloves onboard. The *Trinidad* begins to leak. Almost a year after leaving the Moluccas, the *Vittoria* arrives back in Spain. It is the first ship to circumnavigate the globe.

AROUND THE WORLD

In the early sixteenth century, much of the world was unknown to Europeans, and there were many erroneous ideas about its land and seas.

This modern photograph shows Sugar Loaf Mountain at the entrance to Rio de Janeiro's bay in Brazil, where Magellan anchored for two weeks. The local people thought Magellan's fleet brought the rain because until its arrival, there had been a water shortage that lasted for months.

It was not Magellan's dream to sail around the world. His goal was to reach the Spice Islands, or the Moluccas, by sailing west across the Atlantic, rather than east. He believed this route would involve a much shorter trip.

Most navigators of his day would have agreed with him. By the early part of the sixteenth century, it was generally accepted that the world was round, not flat. Almost everyone, however, thought Earth was only half the size it actually is. Even when explorers found the continents of North and South America, the land that stood in the way of proceeding westward, no one realized at first that they ran north to south almost from pole to pole.

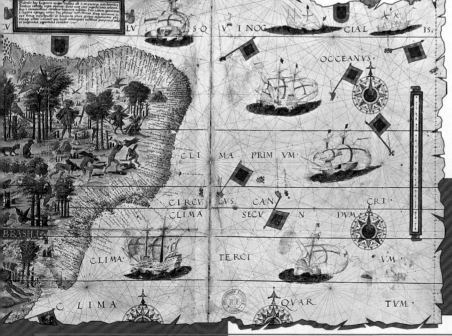

Dating from 1519, the year Magellan set out on his expedition, this map shows the Brazilian coast along which he sailed. Brazil was known as Verzin at the time.

SEEKING A PASSAGE

Convinced there had to be at least one sea passage through the land mass, Magellan thought that the Spice Islands would be only a few days' sailing away once it had been navigated. Not only did Magellan believe that such a route would be much shorter, he also probably thought it would keep the route to the Spice Islands in the hemisphere of the globe that had been awarded to his backer, Spain, by the 1494 Treaty of Tordesillas.

Throughout the fifteenth century, the spice trade lay behind a tremendous rivalry between Spain and Portugal. Pepper, cloves, sandalwood, and cinnamon were all highly sought after. If a new, speedy route to them could be found, there were huge profits to be made. Amazingly, the selling price of certain spices in Northern Europe could easily be ten thousand times greater than the amount paid to growers in the Spice islands of the East Indies.

MAKING HEADWAY

This picture (above) shows the discovery in 1520 of the passage through to the west coast of South America, known as the Strait of Magellan. Who really inspired this voyage, and what sort of navigational instruments were used in the course of the expedition?

A huge statue stands on the waterfront at Lisbon, Portugal, today, erected in memory of a prince who died in 1460. Henry the Navigator encouraged the subsequent Portuguese excellence at sea. Henry was a scholar, and he knew the leading mapmakers of the age. He also set up a school that taught navigation.

Magellan had to rely on four main instruments to guide his ships at sea. The cross-staff, which was used to calculate latitude (the distance north or south of the equator), was made of two main pieces at right angles to each other. One piece was held to the eye while the other was moved up and down until

it filled the gap between the horizon and the polestar. The angle on a scale engraved on the sliding bar could be read to determine the latitude.

The ship's compass was also an important instrument, as was the hourglass, a vital means of measuring time. The most boring job onboard undoubtedly belonged to the unlucky individuals, usually the most junior of the crew, who had to turn the hourglass over each time the sand ran out. Sometimes, in an attempt to alleviate the tedium, those on duty would secretly warm the glass so that it expanded, causing the sand to run through it more speedily than normal.

The nocturnal (above) was an instrument used for telling time during hours of darkness. Through careful observation of the polestar through a hole at the center of the device — around which were two concentric circles, the larger marked with the months of the year and the smaller with the hours of the day — the crew could tell time at night.

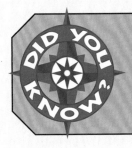

DID YOU KNOW?

Magellan's expedition was financed by the Spanish government. In return for funding the journey, the government expected a large share of the profits. Both Magellan and the government were eager to find a speedy route to the Spice Islands and to improve trade.

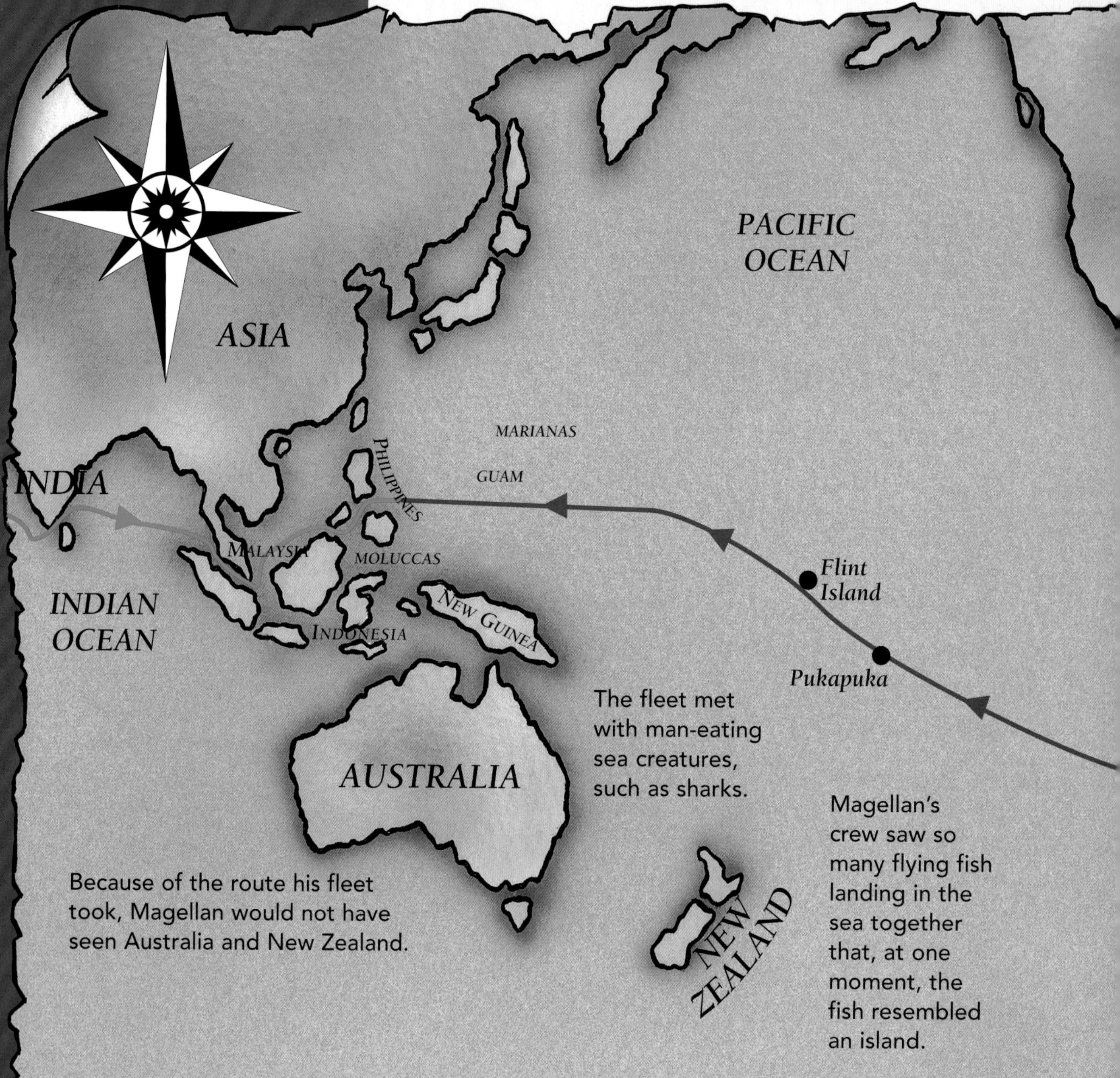

PACIFIC
OCEAN

ASIA

MARIANAS

GUAM

PHILIPPINES

INDIA

MALAYSIA

MOLUCCAS

INDIAN
OCEAN

INDONESIA

NEW GUINEA

Flint
Island

Pukapuka

AUSTRALIA

The fleet met
with man-eating
sea creatures,
such as sharks.

Magellan's
crew saw so
many flying fish
landing in the
sea together
that, at one
moment, the
fish resembled
an island.

Because of the route his fleet
took, Magellan would not have
seen Australia and New Zealand.

NEW ZEALAND

MAGELLAN'S
VOYAGE AROUND THE WORLD

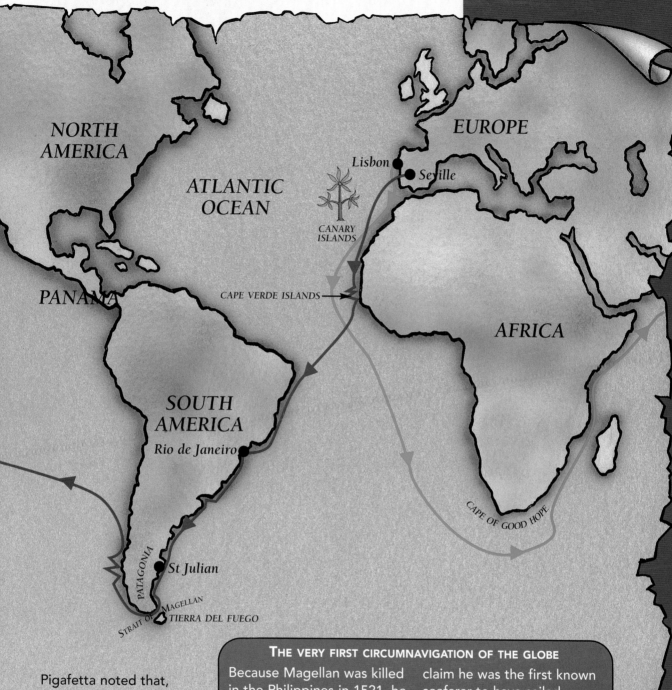

NORTH AMERICA

EUROPE

ATLANTIC OCEAN

Lisbon

Seville

CANARY ISLANDS

PANAMA

CAPE VERDE ISLANDS →

AFRICA

SOUTH AMERICA

Rio de Janeiro

CAPE OF GOOD HOPE

PATAGONIA

St Julian

STRAIT OF MAGELLAN

TIERRA DEL FUEGO

Pigafetta noted that, during summer in this region, there was hardly any night, while in the winter, there was as few as three hours of daylight.

THE VERY FIRST CIRCUMNAVIGATION OF THE GLOBE

Because Magellan was killed in the Philippines in 1521, he was unable to complete the voyage begun in 1519 and return to Seville with his few surviving crew members in 1522. By showing Magellan's two great journeys, this map shows why some historians claim he was the first known seafarer to have sailed around the world. For that era, it was an amazing feat.

KEY
— 1505-1512
— 1519-1522

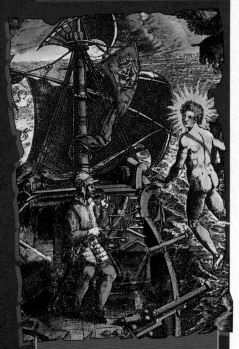

TOWARD NEW HORIZONS

In 1518, Magellan was offered the chance to equip a fleet and sail it west, across the Atlantic, to the Moluccas, also known as the Spice Islands, where fortunes could be made.

This image shows Magellan on his flagship and a symbolic angel at his side. As Pigafetta wrote: "The captain desired that his ship should proceed before the other vessels . . . and for this he carried by night . . . a torch of burning wood . . . so that they should not lose sight of him. . . . When he wanted to change course, he showed two lights."

This detail from a 15th-century fresco shows the sort of pack animals once used for transporting spices and other goods. Such overland journeys were frequently fraught with dangers. A caravan, for example, might have been held up by thieves. Traveling by sea, there was always the risk of pirates.

Magellan went to Spain in 1517, accompanied by Ruy Faliero, a Portuguese geographer. There, the two renounced their Portuguese nationality and offered their services to King Charles I. They proposed a plan for a Spanish expedition to the Spice Islands, which was backed by several influential Spaniards, including Magellan's father-in-law. In March 1518, the king accepted their plan.

The king and Magellan were interested in both exploration and commerce. The king also wanted to extend Spain's power.

In 1517, soon after arriving in Spain, Magellan married Beatriz, daughter of Diego Barbosa, a government official. They shared less than two years of married life, but Magellan was able to see his baby son, Rodrigo (born in late 1518 or early 1519), before setting out on his voyage.

Ignoring everyone else's territorial rights, a pope had issued a decree giving Spain control of all territory lying 370 leagues west of the Cape Verde Islands. If Magellan and Faliero were right, the Spice Islands lay in this area. The king sought to claim the islands for Spain, agreeing to share any profits from the voyage with Magellan and to make him governor of any newly conquered lands.

> ❝ *He did not entirely declare the voyage he was to make, lest men should not, from amazement or fear, be willing to accompany him on so long a voyage.* ❞
> PIGAFETTA

With persuasion from Cardinal Juan Rodriguez de Fonseca, the king granted Magellan the Royal Charter necessary for such an expedition to proceed, made Magellan commander of the fleet, and ordered his officials to provide five ships at the port of Seville.

Preparations for the voyage were sometimes difficult. Many proud Spaniards were concerned that the captain general of the expedition was Portuguese. Magellan and the Spanish government compromised; most of the fleet's ships had Spanish captains but Portuguese pilots. Another problem occurred when Portuguese agents who regarded Magellan as a traitor tried to sabotage the voyage before it even began.

Expeditions are only successful if well planned, and it is believed that Magellan supervised every aspect of the voyage. This meant supervising the fitting out of the five ships that made up the fleet, which took 18 months. Magellan is thought to have been an immensely thorough man, as happy to immerse himself in details as to consider the grandest of plans.

CARGO

We know exactly what sort of cargo, in addition to provisions and seafaring supplies, the five ships of Magellan's expedition carried because records of it have been preserved over the centuries. Obviously intended to be traded for spices such as cloves or vegetables such as red plantains from Malacca (*below*), the cargo included among other items: a large quantity of mercury, 10,000 bundles of cloth, 500 pounds (227 kilograms) of crystals, 5,000 knives, 1,000 mirrors, 10,000 fishhooks, 1,500 combs, and 600 pairs of scissors. The largest, heaviest, and most valuable of items among the cargo was undoubtedly the 20,000 pounds (9,100 kg) of copper. This metal was highly prized in the East Indies, where it was used to make bowls and coins.

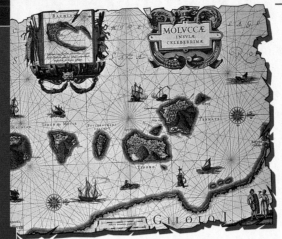

This European map of the Moluccas — the so-called Spice Islands, located in eastern Indonesia — was made after Magellan's voyage. The islands' principal exports included dyes, sandalwood, coconut products, pepper, and as would be expected, a huge variety of spices.

In the many waters through which he sailed while circumnavigating the globe, Magellan would have found fish that were completely new to European eyes — such as these sweetlips, for example.

Magellan may have also traded in spices from India, such as cardamom, the queen of spices, and also the Canary Islands' capers (right), used for flavoring fish, pasta, sauces, and pickles.

The ships themselves were small, old, and in need of a lot of refurbishment before Magellan was satisfied they were capable of the journey.

An even bigger problem was finding competent sailors to man them. The whole trip was shrouded in great secrecy, and few were prepared to sign on for a minimum period of two years without being told where they would be going.

Because of this, Magellan turned a blind eye to rules about the number of Portuguese allowed to sail aboard the Spanish ships. Thirty-seven of the crew were Portuguese, but many others from Portugal joined up using false Spanish names. Thirty Italians and nineteen Frenchmen also served aboard, together with a few Greeks, Flemish, Germans, and a number of slaves. There was just one Englishman who joined the expedition. He was Andrew of Bristol, a gunner who was married to a Spanish woman and had lived in Spain for several years.

Many of the men aboard the ships were not sailors but servants to the Spanish captains. It is known that one of these captains, the aristocratic Cartagena, had no fewer than ten servants to look after his personal needs.

The fleet is thought to have carried two chaplains, five barbers (who also did primitive surgery), and a notary who acted as a lawyer. An astrologer also sailed on the flag-ship. Superstitions were common in Magellan's day.

Each ship had a cook; a chief steward; a carpenter;

and a blacksmith; a caulker, a man whose job it was to keep the timbers watertight; and a cooper, who made and repaired barrels.

Some people aboard the ships were not there to work. One such passenger was Antonio Francesco Pigafetta, a Venetian writer who was curious "to see the wonders

> ❝ *The captain [Magellan] would not allow any women onboard.*
>
> PIGAFETTA ❞

of the world" but who may have been a spy. He kept a journal that survives as the most detailed record of Magellan's expedition.

Because Magellan had no

Magellan called the group of islands shown on this map from about 1570 the Archipelago of St. Lazarus. After his time, maps started to feature lines that told sailors how to steer their ships.

clear idea of where they might find supplies along the route, he aimed to provision his ships with enough equipment to last for two and a half years. Because of wholesale fraud and pilfering at the dockside, however, his fleet set sail with supplies barely sufficient for one year.

At last, on September 20, 1519, having prayed for God's blessing, the ships left the port at San Lucar de Barrameda with cannons blazing. The fleet included the *Trinidad,* Magellan's 130-ton flagship; the *San Antonio,* also 130 tons; the 60-ton Santiago; and the *Vittoria* and *Concepción*, at 90 tons each.

Many locals living in Philippine towns like the one shown below converted to Christianity in the years following Magellan's voyage.

Many peoples in Indonesia and the Philippines built houses on stilts (*left*) that stood far above the swampy ground and out of reach of the wild animals found in the mountain regions. Like the houses shown here, they were made of wood and featured walls of woven rattan or grass.

TO UNCHARTED LANDS

The past is recorded in more ways than just in books and paintings. This corner of a magnificent Persian carpet, made in fourteen colors and now kept in a museum in Vienna, Austria, is an interesting document in its own right. It shows the landing of Portuguese ships with European crews, but it is not known which particular voyage is depicted.

According to a legend, when Magellan arrived at the Canary Islands, he received a message rushed to him aboard a pinnace. It was not good news.

The message is said to have contained information that the King of Portugal — Manuel, who had refused to support Magellan's plans — had sent a large war fleet to intercept the expedition.

Magellan may have changed course to throw them off the scent. For some time, he hugged the coast of West Africa, possibly thinking this would help avoid conflict with the Portuguese.

This map — drawn on vellum by Battista Agnese and once owned by Charles V — traces the world voyage of Magellan's ship. Note that Australia and New Zealand, which were not yet known to Europeans at the time the map was made, are not shown at all. The position of these large land masses in the southern hemisphere was eventually found by Captain Cook and the crew of the *Endeavour* in the eighteenth century.

This change of course led Magellan's fleet into huge thunderstorms and violent seas off Sierra Leone. In evading the Portuguese, Magellan also had to sail into an area where no mariner ever wanted to find himself — the Doldrums. For three weeks, men groaned in the heat, meat went rotten, and the water and wine barrels split and leaked.

> **If our Lord and the Virgin Mother had not helped by giving us fine weather so we could replenish our provisions and other things, we would surely have perished in this very great sea.**
> PIGAFETTA

It is hardly surprising that tempers frayed and men began to question the wisdom of the commander of the fleet. Luckily, however, the current soon carried the ships into trade winds from the southeast. The sails filled, and once more, they were back on course.

The island Magellan called St. Paul's Island may originally have been called Pukapuka by the locals, while what were called the Spice Islands are also known as the Moluccas. Guam and Rota are part of the Marianas, which Magellan called the Ladrones Islands, or the Isles of Thieves.

Two days later, the coast of Brazil appeared on the horizon. The pope had declared Brazil Portuguese territory, and Magellan had no way of knowing whether the Portuguese fleet might be lying in wait for him there. Continuing southwest, after about ten weeks at sea, on the feast day of St. Lucy, Magellan and his ships entered the great harbor that he named Bay Santa Lucia, at a spot known today as Rio de Janeiro. The ships were promptly beached and repaired in a process known as careening.

With holds full of new supplies and barrels of fresh water, the fleet put to sea on Christmas Eve 1519. All that remained now was to find the fabled passage — a route Magellan thought would take them to the Spice Islands after just a few days' sailing.

Although elephants had been known in Europe since Roman times, much exotic wildlife remained unfamiliar to Europeans in the early 16th century.

This detail from a painting in the Naval Museum in Madrid, Spain, shows one of the native people of Patagonia described by Pigafetta as giants.

MATTERS OF FAITH

Magellan lived in an age when most Christians believed that the faith they followed was the only true religion and that anyone of another religion was a heretic.

Today, we would also be amazed at any world leader suddenly announcing he had split up the globe between two great powers. People would ask by what right anyone could make such a declaration. But that is exactly what Pope Adrian VI did in the late fifteenth century. So certain was he that he was not just God's representative on Earth but God's *only* representative on Earth that he had no problem simply drawing a line on the map that was 370 leagues west of the Cape Verde Islands and declaring that everything east of that line belonged to Portugal and everything west of the line belonged to Spain. He believed that in doing this he was carrying out the will of God.

Many explorers regarded the native peoples they met on their travels as savages or, as Pigafetta, the chronicler of Magellan's voyage, called them, "heathens." It was expected that European explorers should try to convert such people to Christianity.

Unfortunately, this effort sometimes had tragic consequences. The overenthusiastic Spanish conquistadors even massacred hundreds of thousands of innocent South American Indians in the name of Christ.

In a similar case, such was the certainty with which some Christians affirmed their faith that, when the Portuguese killed the entire Arab population of Goa in 1510, their viceroy sent an official report to the King of Portugal. In it, he gave thanks for Almighty God's help in the murders.

It is thought, however, that Magellan, who was present at the time, strongly disapproved of such behavior.

Saintly Ways

Magellan had a habit of giving the names of saints to the places he discovered, and on his ships, religious services were frequent. A special Mass was always celebrated at key moments on a voyage.

On Magellan's ships, thanksgiving was particularly fervent when the fleet had met with danger and survived. The priests were well equipped. One item in the fleet's cargo was a large quantity of church candles.

Charles, King of Castile and later Holy Roman Emperor, approved of Magellan's plans and gave support to his proposed voyage.

Religious zeal was in many ways responsible for Magellan's early death. When he arrived in the Philippines, he vigorously set about trying to convert the local people to Christianity. Many said they wanted to become Christians, and among them was the powerful Rajah of Cebu, who was baptized, along with his many wives.

When the Rajah told Magellan that some chiefs on an outlying island had chosen not to give up their heathen gods, however, Magellan took it upon himself to punish them. He was killed while trying to carry out this punishment.

Magellan's religious influence has long continued. Indeed, the Philippines is the only major Catholic region in the Far East today.

On April 14, 1521, Humabon, the Rajah of Cebu, was baptized in a ceremony (*above*) following Magellan's visit to his island and efforts to convert the native people to Christianity.

An intensive search of the area in which it was claimed the entrance to the passage lay proved unsuccessful. Magellan now reasoned that the passage had to lie due south — in waters where no European had ever sailed.

> **We are about to stand into an ocean where no ship has ever sailed before. May the ocean always be as calm and benevolent as it is today. In this hope I name it the Pacific Ocean.**
>
> MAGELLAN

The waters around the tip of South America are among the most dangerous in the world. For eight whole weeks, the fleet battled against storms. When winter was at its worst, Magellan called a halt, stopping the fleet in Patagonia, one of the bleakest spots on earth, where they waited for spring. More troubling, they were running short of food. Rations were cut, and the men grew disgruntled.

Shortly afterward, the smallest ship, the *Santiago*, was destroyed in a storm, but all except one of the men were saved. Strangely, it was a storm that finally put the expedition on the right track. Two ships, the *San Antonio* and the *Concepción,* seemed to have disappeared. Magellan was astounded when, after rounding a promontory, he met up with them again. This time, they were flying every flag they possessed, having discovered the fabled passage, later named the Strait of Magellan. The passage is a series of connected channels broken by islands. Along the shoreline, Magellan saw the campfires of native peoples and gave the area the name it has to this day — *Tierra del Fuego,* or "land of fire." The ships would soon be sailing through the strait and into the Pacific Ocean.

Magellan no doubt saw many extraordinary reptiles in the places that he visited during his travels.

Melaka, visited by Magellan during his years of sailing on behalf of Portugal, was and still is home to many amazing forms of wildlife, including the flying squirrel (*above*).

Before he disembarked at Melaka, Magellan is unlikely to have seen a creature like the long-snouted tapir (*right*).

FRIENDS OR FOES?

Henry the Navigator, who founded a Portuguese school of navigation, may have greatly influenced Magellan and others.

Duke Manuel (*above*), who became king of Portugal, was not willing to support Magellan, leading Magellan to offer his services to Spain.

A number of people gave Magellan the idea of going to sea, and a few came to his aid. One even kept a detailed diary of his voyage. Others, however, stood in his way.

By the time of Magellan's death in the Philippines, his fleet had been reduced to three vessels and only 120 of the original crew of 270. Juan Lopez Carvalho, who had taken command, decided to burn one of the ships, the *Concepción*, because there was simply not sufficient manpower to sail it. But it was not just this ship that was burned. Carvalho is also thought to have ordered every single one of Magellan's papers — his logs, his diary, his letters — to be destroyed.

Carvalho may have realized that Magellan, a thorough man, would have recorded every single detail of his expedition — including the mutinies and lack of discipline, particularly among the Spanish — and these were not the sort of stories he wanted told.

As a boy, Magellan was a page at the court of Queen Leonor of Portugal, who is shown as a young woman in this detail from a painting (*right*). Leonor was the spouse of the Portuguese sovereign known as King John the Perfect. After King John was poisoned, Duke Manuel came to the throne.

Antonio Pigafetta, a Venetian nobleman who had signed on with Magellan's fleet so that he could see the wonders of the world, however, guarded his diary carefully and had it published when he got home. It survives today.

I determined to experience and to go, that it might be told that I made the voyage and saw with my eyes the things hereafter written, and that I might win a famous name.
PIGAFETTA

Pigafetta, an educated and cultured man, was in his early twenties in 1519. Magellan may not have welcomed Pigafetta because he did not want "tourists" aboard his ships. Pigafetta, however, grew to respect Magellan greatly. It may also have been a bonus for the commander to find that Pigafetta was a born reporter.

DAILY TASK

Because, as a volunteer, Pigafetta had no particular duties aboard, his time was his own, and he filled it by keeping a detailed account of day-to-day happenings. He was rarely seen without his notebook in hand.

Pigafetta, it seems, was also, a talented linguist, the sort of person who, with a few days' practice, could pick up enough of almost any tongue to make himself understood. We know, for example, that he acquired a working knowledge of Malay, an Indonesian language.

Questions remain about Pigafetta, however. Some historians claim he may have been a Venetian spy, sent to keep an eye on expanding Spanish trade with the East. If so, he disguised the reason for his presence well. Without his account begun in 1519, we would not have nearly as much information about Magellan's voyage.

TEAM SPIRIT

- If necessary, Magellan was not too proud to lend a hand to help out his crew, despite his own physical challenges and the demands of commanding the fleet.

- According to some accounts, during the crossing of the Pacific, the barber aboard Magellan's flagship, the *Trinidad*, died of scurvy. This was a blow because a ship's barber did much more than trim beards; he was also the ship's surgeon and a medical auxiliary. It is said that Magellan took on these duties without complaint. Every morning, he visited the sick and supervised the preparation of a gruel of biscuit crumbs. He also instructed that even maggots be boiled up to provide extra nourishment for the men.

- Later, Magellan stopped at the island of Guam, where the abundance of fresh fruit and pure water helped some of the sick to recover.

- In 1509, Magellan risked his life to save his cousin, Francisco Serrano, from being harmed by the Sultan of Melaka.

King John of Portugal, like his great uncle Henry the Navigator, supported maritime adventures before he was assassinated.

In 1505, Magellan joined a very large Portuguese fleet under Francisco d'Almeida (*right*), Viceroy of India. After his son's murder, d'Almeida massacred the citizens of Dabul and fought a huge Arab fleet in a battle that caused heavy losses to both sides.

Taken from a sixteenth-century book now in the Pierpont Morgan Library in New York, this illustration shows the fleet of Francisco d'Almeida.

TALL STORY?

In the course of the voyage, Pigafetta saw many exotic places and peoples, just as he had set out to do. During the search for the Strait of Magellan, for example, there appeared on the shore one day a figure he described as that of ". . . a huge giant who was naked and who danced, leaped and sang. He was so tall that even the largest of us came only to midway between his waist and his shoulder."

Magellan named this race of giants *Patagones*, or "big feet" in Spanish. To this day, that region of South America is known as Patagonia — or, in translation, "land of the big feet."

Pigafetta was fascinated by these people and wrote at length about their customs, among which was an unusual and unpleasant medical procedure. "When these giants have a pain in the stomach," Pigafetta wrote, "instead of taking medicine they put down their throat an arrow two feet or thereabout in length, then they vomit of a green color mingled with blood."

According to Pigafetta, the reason the vomit was green was that the Patagonians often ate thistles. Perhaps it was these that gave them stomachaches.

> ❝ *No one had such...courage or learning.*
> PIGAFETTA
> ON MAGELLAN ❞

Although some aspects of these tales are hard to believe, some people think that these Patagonian "giants" did once exist. Pigafetta said they were about 7 feet 5 inches (226 centimeters) in height — far taller than most fully grown men today.

Sir Francis Drake, a British admiral who came across them years later, confirmed their unusual appearance. In spite of this further sighting, these very tall Patagonians seem to have vanished off the face of the Earth. No one

During his years in India, Magellan also served under the command of Alfonso de Albuquerque.

Columbus (*top left*) undoubtedly inspired Magellan (*bottom left*). Amerigo Vespucci and Francisco Pizarro are the other explorers shown around the map (*below*).

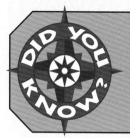

Pigafetta recorded a number of words from several of the languages he came across on the voyage. In the language of the Patagonians, for example, he explained that *oli* meant water; *capac* meant bread; *pelpeli* meant gold; a dog was a *holl*; and *haisi!* signified "come here!"

knows what could have happened to them.

Pigafetta's journals are also full of vivid descriptions of the lands Magellan's expedition visited. "In the land of Cimbombom," ever-observant Pigafetta tells us, there were "certain trees, the leaves of which, when they fall to the ground, become alive and walk." That may sound like pure fantasy, but in fact he was describing the behavior of creatures known as stick insects. No European had previously written about these fascinating creatures that mimic the appearance of foliage and twigs in a superb example of camouflage.

Pigafetta's description of scurvy is also highly accurate, and he thanked God that he did not suffer from it himself. It appears that Pigafetta was not only a great reporter but also was capable of tolerating the rigors of the long voyage.

Like Magellan, Pigafetta regarded the people they discovered as heathens and was delighted when they freely asked to convert to Christianity. "Each of us

wept for joy we had at the good-will of those people. . . . The captain told them that . . . if they wished to become Christians, it should be with a good heart and a love of God. Then all cried out together with one voice that they wished to become Christians of their own free will."

Ever loyal to Magellan, Pigafetta wrote that "no one else had so much natural wit, courage or learning to sail once round the world as he had undertaken." His diaries have also ensured a record of Magellan's contribution to European exploration.

STAYING ALIVE AT SEA

Magellan had to overcome mutiny, desertion, and sickness among his crew. The biggest problem, however, was that no one realized the size of the Pacific Ocean.

Juan de Cartagena (*above*) was the captain of one of Magellan's ships. Cartagena was involved in two plots of mutiny, but Magellan stood firm through both. Magellan spared Cartagena's life following the first mutiny, but after the second mutiny, he decided to maroon Cartagena on the Patagonian coast.

On several occasions, Magellan had to face severe storms. The current was so forceful that it was impossible for the ship to maintain its course. Pigafetta even reported that at times, all aboard the ships were in tears, expecting that death would overtake them.

Right from the outset, some of Magellan's crew conspired to undermine his authority. The pinnace that reached Magellan's fleet while in the Canary Islands during the early weeks of the voyage also carried a message from his father-in-law that three Spanish captains were planning to murder him. Led by the treacherous Juan de Cartagena, the captains are believed to have planned a meeting with Magellan during which they were hoping to provoke the commander into a fight and stab him.

TAKEN BY SURPRISE

At the start of the meeting, the captains made certain demands. Aware of the plot against him, Magellan agreed to what they wanted. Outmaneuvered and with no reason to fight, the captains returned to their own ships. But if they believed that, from then on, Magellan would take their orders, they were very mistaken. Just two days after leaving the Canary Islands, Magellan changed course from the one decided upon at the meeting with the captains. He is thought to have done so to evade the Portuguese fleet. When Cartagena sailed to the flagship to protest at this change of route, Magellan simply announced that he was to follow him and ask no questions whatsoever.

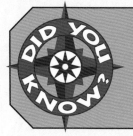
Pigafetta recorded that twenty-nine crew members died of scurvy during the long journey across the Pacific. Scurvy is a disease caused by the lack of vitamin C. Its symptoms include spongy gums, loosening of the teeth, and bleeding into the skin and mucous membranes.

> **No longer am I prepared to follow the hazardous course set by a fool.**
> CARTAGENA

Later, when the Spanish captains came to Magellan's flagship to attend a court martial, they appeared fully armed and wanted to use the occasion to take control.

It was mutiny! Magellan signaled for the armed men waiting outside to enter the cabin. Cartagena ordered the captains to stab Magellan but was immediately over-powered, dragged across the deck, and placed in the stocks. Although it was within Magellan's rights to behead Cartagena then and there, instead, he removed the traitor from command of the *San Antonio* and imprisoned him, later releasing the traitor on parole.

This was not to be the only mutiny. While Magellan's fleet was wintering in Patagonia, trouble started once again.

According to Pigafetta, one of the Canary Islands had no water source except a cloud that descended once a day onto a large tree. Water was distilled from this tree's fallen leaves.

This image (*left*) shows Magellan's entire fleet shortly after leaving Seville, Spain. The five vessels were the *Trinidad*, which was his flagship; the *San Antonio*; the *Concepción*; the *Santiago*; and the *Vittoria*, which was the only vessel of the fleet to return safely — against all odds — to Europe.

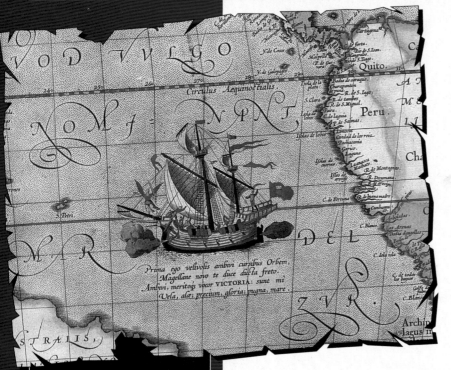

Magellan's ship, the *Vittoria*, is featured in this detail from the map on page 40. By July 1520, the few surviving crew members had run out of water and food. Fishermen took pity on the men and gave them supplies. The ship itself, meanwhile, was hardly in a fit state to sail. Despite its poor condition, the *Vittoria* was the one ship of the fleet that made it back to Spain.

Whenever supplies ran dangerously low on their extended voyage, Magellan and the crew of his fleet had to rely on the exotic seafood that they could catch, such as giant-sized crabs (*right*) and sharks.

The officers, particularly the Spaniards, had suggested returning to calmer waters, an idea supported by an overwhelming majority. Magellan did not agree to their suggestion. The stage was set for further trouble, and it started aboard the *Concepción*. By silently boarding two other ships during the night, Cartagena's mutineers found themselves in control of the *San Antonio*

and the *Vittoria*. Luckily for Magellan, however, the *Vittoria* dragged her anchor, all but collided with his flagship, and was soon back under his control. The mutiny had collapsed.

Luis de Mendoza, one of the three captains, had been killed during the skirmish; another captain, Gaspar de Quesada, was executed for the murder of a man loyal to Magellan.

Cartagena was sentenced to be marooned ashore on the bleak Patagonian coast with a mutinous priest to keep him company — a death sentence for both of them. The rest of the mutineers were originally sentenced to death, too, but Magellan later changed their punishment to hard labor.

FARAWAY PLACES

After the ships sailed through the passage now known as the Strait of Magellan and entered the Pacific Ocean, Magellan believed that, with a couple of days' gentle sailing, they would reach the Spice Islands. It was not long, however, before he began to worry. He could see the west coast of South America to his right, but there was no sign of the east coast.

Magellan is thought to have reasoned that Asia was

Magellan's expedition was not strictly a military venture, but he knew there might be times when weapons would be necessary. He therefore sailed with a large quantity of gunpowder; over 70 cannons; and 50 harquebuses, which were heavy, portable guns, usually fired from supports.

slightly further away than anyone thought. Following the trade winds, he changed course and sailed toward the northwest. Although he was right, Asia was not to be found just over the horizon as Magellan anticipated. It was actually thousands of miles away.

> **The fool is leading us to destruction. On the flame of his ambition, he will crucify us all.**
> <small>CARTAGENA</small>

Although he had no way of knowing it, Magellan had chosen one of the worst possible moments to change course. Had he done so a few days earlier, he would have found Easter Island, which would have led him to a series of small islands where there was abundant food and fresh water. But even from the tops of the masts, his lookouts could not see far.

ESCAPING DISASTER

Soon the water in the barrels turned yellow and stank so badly that men could only drink it by holding their noses. Daily rationing was then introduced, and the sailors received just six ounces of worm-infested biscuits a day. Rats were now on the menu, too.

In fury, Magellan threw his charts into the sea. They had proved useless. He had to carry on anyway, hoping to find land before his whole crew perished in the vast sea.

Finally, on January 24, 1521, they spotted a tiny island, but it had no edible vegetation and, critically, no fresh water. Fortunately, though, it began to rain, allowing them to fill the water barrels. After about a week, they had also filled the holds with supplies of smoked shark flesh and turtle eggs, and they put to sea again. Magellan felt certain their voyage was nearly over. Little did he realize, however, that there was still a huge expanse of ocean to be crossed.

WEATHER REPORT

Conditions may have been desperate for the men during the long voyage across the Pacific, but at least they suffered few problems from the weather. This is why Magellan gave this sea its name, derived from the word "peaceful." As Pigafetta wrote in his journal, "During these three months and twenty days, we sailed across the Pacific Sea, which is rightly so named. For, during this time, we had no storm."

This was in sharp contrast to the kind of weather the fleet had encountered while sailing in the Atlantic Ocean. Pigafetta has also left us a vivid picture of conditions there, describing ". . . wind and currents which came head-on to us so that we could not advance. . . ."

MASSACRES, GOLD, AND PLUNDER

The *Vittoria, above,* was the only vessel from Magellan's original fleet of five to arrive safely back in Spain.

In 1510, the Portuguese massacred the Muslims living in Goa. Magellan is believed not to have taken part in the killings.

Magellan and his crew faced many difficult moments but believed they had been saved by the discovery of an island. When they moved toward it, doubts arose.

At dawn on March 6, 1521, a lookout in the crow's nest aboard the *Trinidad* scanned the horizon and could not believe his eyes. Ahead lay an island, and the closer they sailed to it, the more clearly everyone aboard could see a small, sandy inlet with a village of thatched houses.

Next morning, the *Trinidad* entered the bay and dropped anchor. It is thought that within moments, the ship was surrounded by a fleet of manned canoes and that each islander was armed with a stone knife, a wooden spear, and a club. To Magellan's weakened crew, the islanders must have seemed menacing, and they soon set about looting the flagship, taking anything they could carry,

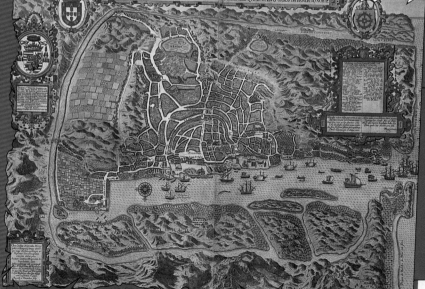

This picture shows the port of Goa, India, which came under Portuguese control. Magellan was chosen by Alfonso d'Albuquerque — the Viceroy of India — to command one of the viceroy's ships and probably took part in the capture of the city.

> **The greatest commodity in that island is an abundance of gold. They showed us certain small valleys, making signs to us that there was as much gold there as they had hairs, but they had no iron or tools to mine it.**
>
> PIGAFETTA

especially metal objects.

This may have looked like deliberate theft, but it is thought to have been pure curiosity. What Magellan did not know was that these people — the Chamorros of Guam — were a race brought up to believe they were superior to everyone else. Fit and healthy themselves, they had little respect for the strangers, many of whom had not enough strength to stand.

Things are said to have really gone wrong when Magellan ordered the natives to give back what they had taken and leave. When they did not obey, Magellan's men opened fire with crossbows. The deck was quickly covered in bodies, and the remaining islanders fled the ship, taking its skiff with them. There was no chance now of trading with the islanders for the food and water Magellan's men badly needed.

STOLEN GOODS

As Magellan's ships sailed past the village the next morning, each let loose a broadside of cannon fire, and Magellan watched as the terrified islanders ran away to the hills. With men on guard in case of a surprise attack, his crew now raided the village's storehouses, carrying off everything they could snatch, including pigs, chickens, yams, coconuts, and bananas, and filling their water casks from the river.

They then put to sea, fearing more trouble. Before long, a whole flotilla of canoes approached and surrounded the fleet.

Magellan ordered his cannons to be loaded with stones in case the natives tried to board, but they did not. The supplies the crew had seized were welcome, but there was enough for only a few days. To obtain more, they sailed to the nearby island of Rota.

Magellan survived attack at Melaka (*above*) in 1509, where he also rescued his cousin.

Most of the time, Magellan coped admirably with his adversaries and all sorts of difficulties.

Magellan wed the daughter of wealthy Diego Barbosa.

Magellan named the *Mar Pacifico* — in translation, the Pacific Ocean.

The strait bearing Magellan's name was discovered during his voyage.

Many types of parrots, some of which were said to have been able to speak, were reported to exist in the Spice Islands.

Magellan may have extracted dragon tree sap while in the Canary Islands, his first stopping point after leaving Spain. The sap was thought to be a cure for many ailments.

Pigafetta wrote that wild llamas, like those shown here, were killed and eaten by locals in Patagonia. He described the animals as a cross between a mule and a camel.

STRIKING A BARGAIN

Magellan could have simply raided Rota, firing his cannons, and taking what he wanted. But one of the Chamorros had survived, and Magellan asked him to interpret, telling the Rota islanders that his men meant no harm and were eager to trade knives and axes for food. Magellan set a generous exchange rate, and by the evening, the trading concluded, his ships were back at sea. It is even recorded that the islander was so impressed that he joined Magellan's ship as a full-time interpreter.

It was some time since Magellan had met first with the Portuguese sovereign and then with the Spanish king. He found himself in royal company again when he landed on another island and received a visit from the local rajah, Colambu.

Magellan and Colambu are even said to have performed a ritual that made them blood-brothers.

> ## *For metal, iron, and other large wares, they gave us gold, and for the other and meaner goods, rice, pigs, goods and other provisions.*
>
> PIGAFETTA

What interested Magellan's crew most of all, however, was that the rajah obviously had lots of gold. Strangely, he also seemed perfectly willing to exchange this gold for their iron. A rate of exchange was set — one pound of gold for one pound of iron.

With this rajah's help, Magellan then sailed for the

island of Cebu, where another rajah, Humabon, had even more gold. Magellan was soon on good terms with him, too.

A NEW ROLE

Magellan now saw himself as the King of Spain's unofficial governor of a large number of new territories. But that was not all. If his duty was to lay the foundation for Spanish control, it seemed to him the most sensible thing to do was convert the islanders to Catholicism.

At first, he was very successful at this, organizing baptism for Humabon (who even became known as the Christian King) and thousands of the locals. But one chief, Cilapulapu, who lived on the nearby island of Mactan, sent a message saying that not only would he and his people continue to hold their old beliefs, they would fight in defense of their right to maintain their original faith. On hearing this, Magellan asked for volunteers to help punish Cilapulapu and his followers.

Led by Magellan, forty-eight of his remaining men, in heavy armor, staggered ashore through water that came up to their waists. Waiting for them were thousands of armed Mactans.

Given the overwhelming odds, the Europeans fought magnificently, but it was a hopeless situation. Forced back into the water, Magellan and a few others tried valiantly to defend the rest of the crew and the ships. While fighting in the shallows, however, Magellan met his death. As Pigafetta put it, "All these people threw themselves on him, and one of them with a large javelin thrust it into his leg."

Magellan's ships are shown here reaching the Ladrones Islands (in translation from Spanish, the Isles of Thieves). They were given this name by Magellan because the natives there stole from his fleet. The actual canoes used by the islanders were different from those shown here.

According to Pigafetta, who described them as poor but ingenious, the inhabitants of the three Islands of Thieves frequently went to sea to catch flying fish, like those shown surrounding a ship in this 16th-century illustration. Both men and women engaged in this task, catching the fish using hooks made from fishbones.

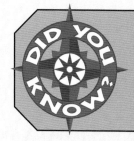

DID YOU KNOW?

Human hair decorating the Chamorros' shields seems to indicate they were cannibals. It is believed that the Guarani people from Rio de Janeiro were cannibalistic, too. They were said to cut their enemies into pieces and eat small, dried morsels daily with ordinary food.

ADDING TO THE MAP

A modern photograph of the stark and sparsely inhabited environment of the Strait of Magellan shows that it is much the same today as it was when first navigated.

The *San Antonio* deserted Magellan's other ships, but Magellan was determined to go on. According to Pigafetta, Magellan wept with joy when his fleet managed to navigate the strait.

Magellan's travels without doubt merit a permanent place in the annals of history. But how valuable did his explorations prove to be?

Circumnavigation of the globe would certainly have silenced once and for all the skeptics who continued to believe that the world is flat.

Magellan and his crew did much more than that. No longer, for example, would the mainland south of the River Plate have to be marked on maps as *terra incognita,* meaning "unknown land" in Latin.

Sailors would also remain grateful for the discovery of the strait bearing Magellan's name. At the tip of South America is the notoriously stormy Cape Horn. Any way of avoiding it when sailing to the other coast of South America is helpful.

Before his voyage, of course, Europeans did not even know that some of the places Magellan visited existed. A number of places were given European names by Magellan, who often named places after the saints on whose days he first explored them. Examples include Cape Santa Maria, the Cape of the Eleven Thousand Virgins, St. Paul's Island, and the Canal of All Saints (known today as the Strait of Magellan).

Not all places Magellan explored have kept the names he gave them, however. The islands called the *Ladrones*, or the Islands of Thieves, by Magellan are today known as the Mariana Islands. They include the islands of Guam and Rota.

A CAPITAL NAME

Names coined by Magellan that are still used in South America include Patagonia, Tierra del Fuego, and one taken from a casual remark that some historians believe Magellan made during the search for a passage in the estuary of the River Plate. "*I see a mountain!*" he is said to have cried — in the original Spanish, "*Monte video!*" "Montevideo" was later adopted as the name for the capital of Uruguay.

> ❝ *Truly, I believe that no such voyage will ever be made again.* ❞
> PIGAFETTA

When Magellan reached the end of the strait that now bears his name, the sheer size and emptiness of the body of water that he named the Pacific Ocean came as a shock. Sailing for weeks but never sighting land, Magellan probably realized that the existing theories about Earth's size had to be wrong. The planet was far bigger than anyone had previously imagined.

As for success at a personal level, we will never know for sure whether Magellan realized that he might have sailed around the world. Although he died before what was left of his fleet made it back to Spain, some historians think that when his fleet got to the island of Samar in the Philippines, Magellan was at a spot he had almost certainly reached by sailing in the other direction as a very young man. All this makes it surprising to some people that Magellan's expedition was not widely hailed as a great success in his own era.

Magellan's fleet would have had to cross the Tropic of Capricorn, which lies south of the equator and is marked on this map. The position of this imaginary line corresponds to the position of the Tropic of Cancer, which lies in the Northern Hemisphere.

The Strait of Magellan (*below*) lies between the island of Tierra del Fuego and the mainland of South America. It is about 330 miles (530 kilometers) long and between 2 and 15 miles (3–24 km) wide. Although less important as a sea route since the building of the Panama Canal in the nineteenth century, the Strait of Magellan is still used by ships to cross from one side of South America to the other.

Magellan named the headland at the Pacific exit to the Strait bearing his name Cape Deseado (in translation from Portuguese, the "longed-for Cape") because, as Pigafetta explains, they had sought this passage from one ocean to the other so eagerly and for a great length of time.

It may seem that Magellan and his crew were cruel to the penguins of the islands near the foot of South America, but the sailors were desperate. The flesh of the flightless birds was eaten, their blubber was used as oil for lamps, and their skins were sewn into clothing.

This detail is taken from a fine, colored pictorial map made in 1606 by the cartographer Jodocus Hondius of Amsterdam, located in the Netherlands. Made about 86 years after the death of Magellan, it shows the South American regions of Patagonia and Tierra del Fuego as well as the famous Strait of Magellan. Compared to modern maps, this one is drawn upside down.

One reason his voyage may not have been appreciated was that, for many years, Magellan's reputation was dragged through the mud by survivors like Juan Sebastian del Cano for their own ends. Magellan also lost favor because the westerly route to the Spice Islands he had set out to find was eventually proven to be longer than sailing directly east from Europe.

Nobody knew this before Magellan made his voyage. Once it became clear what was involved in this particular route, few wanted to follow Magellan's course. It was far too long, far too dangerous, and therefore far too costly.

The fairest conclusion is that Magellan's great adventure was highly successful as a scientific exploration. It added an immense amount to the knowledge people had of Earth at that time.

THE DATE FACTOR

After Magellan's death, a particularly interesting observation was made by the diarist Pigafetta as a result of the expedition.

Pigafetta came to realize that during the voyage, they had somehow lost an entire day. This was astonishing because he had kept very detailed records and had never missed making a daily entry in his log.

The discrepancy first came to light when they sighted the Cape Verde Islands on their way back to Spain. As he wrote, "On Wednesday July 9 [1522], we arrived at one of these islands named

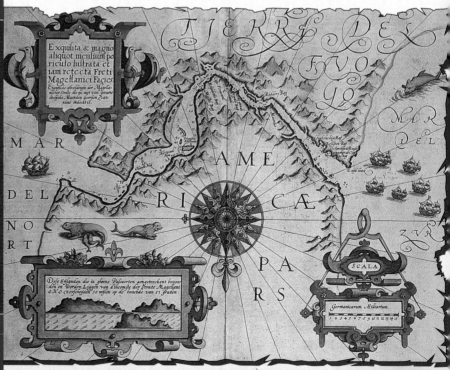

Pigafetta was highly educated for the time, but he must also have had a lot of imagination. He wrote about an island near Java, for example, where there were no men. Women on the island were said to made pregnant by the wind, and if a baby boy was born, they were said to kill him.

Santiago and requested the men who went ashore to enquire what day it was." It was almost as if he had an inkling something was odd. They were all surprised to learn that, "To the Portuguese it was Thursday, which was amazing because to us it was Wednesday and we did not know how we could possibly have made a mistake." Pigafetta continued, "Every day, as I was always in good health, I had written down the date, with no gaps. But as we have been told since, there had been no mistake."

Scientists were later able to offer a simple explanation of what had caused the difference. If you travel west, the day lengthens by one hour for every 15 degrees of longitude, because you are traveling in the same direction as the Sun. The globe is divided into 360 degrees of longitude, which can be divided by 15 degrees into 24 parts. When Pigafetta returned from circumnavigating the globe, he was exactly 24 hours behind local time.

If you travel around the world in an easterly direction, the reverse will be true. You will *gain* one hour for every 15 degrees of longitude traveled. If you continued traveling without altering your watch, you would arrive back one full day *ahead* of the current date at your starting point.

What people really needed to know was where one day ended and the next began. This problem was solved much later, in 1885, by the introduction of the International Date Line, an irregular, imaginary line on the map that runs north to south near the middle of the Pacific Ocean. This line was chosen because very little inhabitable land exists there. When a ship or aircraft crosses the line, a day is dropped from the calendar if going east, and a day is added if going west.

At the very slow pace of a sixteenth-century sailing ship, change in the length of the day evidently went unnoticed. It took one ship sailing all the way around the world before anyone realized that it happened at all.

A LASTING LEGACY

On Earth, Magellan is commemorated by the strait that bears his name. In addition to a space observatory named after him, Magellan's name also lives on in outer space itself! Sailors, especially in the sixteenth century, were very superstitious, and they were liable to interpret any slightly unusual event as an omen. During the crossing of the Pacific, Magellan's crew suddenly noticed new stars in the sky and sought the guidance of the fleet's astrologer as to their significance. He had to admit, however, that these heavenly bodies had never come to his attention before. Later, they were found to be two small galaxies near the Milky Way. One is in the constellation Dorado (Swordfish); the other is in the constellation Tucana (Toucan). In honor of Magellan, the former is now known as the Large Magellanic Cloud, and the latter is called the the Small Magellanic Cloud.

THE JOURNEY HOME

Magellan, the fleet's primary navigator, had been killed, and the remaining crew was still thousands of miles from home. How did they finally make it back to Seville?

Magellan was killed in the Philippines in a conflict with a hostile chieftain. As Pigafetta put it, "With lances of iron and bamboo and javelins, they slew our mirror, our guiding light, our comfort, and our true and only guide."

This highly decorated armor of rattan coated with resin and cowrie shells comes from the Philippines. Over the centuries, tribal chiefs dressed in these suits for ceremonial occasions.

After Magellan's death, command of the fleet was first taken by Duarte Barbosa, the brother-in-law of Magellan and a Spanish captain. Barbosa tried but was unable to recover Magellan's body from the ruler of Mactan. Some historians believe it was this failure that speedily sent the reputation of the Europeans sliding even lower in the estimation of the people of Cebu.

The victory of local warriors over Magellan's heavily armed men was also seen by some as a triumph of traditional religion over Christianity.

Some of the islanders planned an ambush on the Europeans. The Europeans were invited to a farewell banquet, but it was a trap. During an attack, 27 of them, including nearly all the officers, died.

Command now passed to one of the pilots, Carvalho, who seems not to have had the slightest clue how to proceed. It is said by some that Carvalho turned pirate, sailing aimlessly in the South China Sea for many months, plundering and overcoming ship after ship.

Aboard the ship, Carvalho behaved very badly, keeping three unfortunate women locked in his cabin. The crew was soon up in arms, and

Carvalho was relieved of command. In his place, the men elected Gonzales de Espinosa as captain. Espinosa was no skilled navigator either, but he was well-liked, honest, and tough enough to restore discipline aboard the ships.

> ❝ *From the time we first set sail... we had traveled fourteen thousand four hundred and sixty leagues and completed the circuit of the world from East to West.*
>
> PIGAFETTA ❞

Four months later, in November 1521, the two remaining ships arrived in the Moluccas — the Spice Islands. The crews were ecstatic. "It is no wonder we should be so joyful," wrote Pigafetta, "for we had suffered travails and perils for the space of twenty-five months less two days in the search for Molucca."

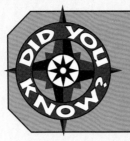

DID YOU KNOW?

When the *Vittoria* was dismasted in a storm, the Spanish crew wanted to surrender to the Portuguese in Mozambique. So seriously, however, did del Cano take the Portuguese threat to a Spanish ship that he said it would be better to die than fall into enemy hands.

Francisco Serrano, who was Magellan's cousin and shipmate in his early travels on the Indian Ocean, had described the Spice Islands as "a New World, richer, greater and more beautiful that that of Vasco da Gama." This description, it was now apparent, was accurate.

There was a warm welcome from the local king, who allowed them to display and sell the cargo they had brought from Spain and to barter for spices.

The sailors stayed for several months. Before departing, they stuffed their holds with all sorts of goods, including cloves and parrots. The *Trinidad* may have been overloaded, however, because it began to leak.

St. Elmo's fire, named after one of the saints who is said to care for seamen, is a luminous discharge that occurs during electrical storms. It was seen during Magellan's voyage and was taken by the crew as a sign that, in spite of severe conditions at sea, they were being protected. Pigafetta wrote that it finally grew very bright, and the sea then grew calm.

Discovery of the Strait of Magellan in 1520 was to help many future expeditions, including that of Charles Darwin, father of the theory of evolution, who sailed to South America in the ship *Beagle*, primarily to research the region's animal life.

This map of the Pacific Ocean by Abraham Ortelius shows New Guinea and South America. It was drawn many years after Magellan's death, but in his honor, it features a picture of the sole surviving ship of his fleet, the *Vittoria*.

Spanish and Portuguese explorers are said to have been nervous about venturing inland from the South American coasts because of what to them at the time were extra-ordinary forms of wildlife. No one knew what kinds of animals they would find. They also didn't know how the local people in those areas would react to them.

Back in the sixteenth century, sailing into uncharted waters — even an ocean as calm as the Pacific — was thought to involve many risks for a captain and his crew, as symbolized by this German woodcut of the period.

Espinosa, the captain of the *Trinidad*, sent the *Vittoria* ahead without him and some of his crew. Sadly, only he and about three of his men made it back to Spain.

Under Juan Sebastian del Cano's command, the sixty men on the *Vittoria* now began sailing the thousands of miles home. It was no smooth journey. They needed fresh food and water, and they also had to avoid capture by the Portuguese, who controlled all the harbors along the route. As for the sailing conditions,

they prayed for fair weather. Finally, after sailing far south, the *Vittoria* was forced to put into the Portuguese-controlled Cape Verde Islands.

The men who went ashore were told that, if approached, they were to say that their foremast had broken. Fisher-men gave them a meal of rice and fresh water, but when the shore party was taken prisoner, del Cano quickly headed out to sea, leaving some of his men behind.

The *Vittoria* reached Seville on September 8, 1522, and the 18 survivors went to give thanks the next day. As Pigafetta wrote, "We all went in our shirts and barefoot, and each holding a torch, to visit the shrine of Santa Maria de la Victoria and that of Santa Maria de Antigua."

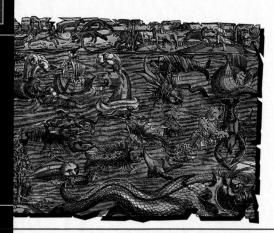

FOR FURTHER DISCUSSION

There are many aspects of Magellan's travels that are thought to be controversial and therefore open to debate. The following questions can be used to guide classroom discussion.

1 Do you think Magellan was totally disloyal to the Portuguese crown? Or should the King of Portugal have done more to support Magellan's claim that it might be possible to sail around the world?

2 Why was the young King of Spain so eager to support Magellan's intended voyage?

3 Was Magellan always as open and truthful as he might have been with his crew? Do you think he was popular with them?

4 Who did Magellan think were his greatest enemies, and why? Was he right? Who proved to be his greatest allies?

5 In which ways could Magellan be considered to have had an unlucky maritime career?

6 What must have surprised Magellan and his crew most about the flora, fauna, and local customs in the various different parts of the world he visited during his expedition?

7 What sort of mistakes, if any, did Magellan make? For what sort of behavior could he rightly be criticized, or was he entirely blameless?

8 Magellan lost his life before he had the chance to make the return journey to Europe. How accurate is it to credit him with being the first to circumnavigate the globe?

9 What were Magellan's best qualities? How good a sea captain did he make?

10 For what do we have to thank Pigafetta? What contribution did he make to Magellan's worldwide and lasting fame?

11 If you had to write a one-sentence epitaph for Magellan, what would it say?

12 Do you think the people of Spain have good reason to celebrate the life of Magellan?

13 To what extent do you think Magellan was a man of his time? What sort of career might best suit someone with his sort of character today?

14 Was Magellan right to try to convert islanders to Catholicism, or should he have let them follow their own faith?

15 Whose fault was it that Magellan died on Mactan Island?

16 Was Magellan more interested in exploration for exploration's sake or making a fortune and a lasting reputation as a seafarer?

MAJOR WORLD EVENTS

The period during which Magellan made his circumnavigation of the world is known by historians as the Golden Age of Exploration. As you will see from the explorations listed here, several European nations were intent on reaching new shores during that era. In several cases, the regimes that sponsored these voyages also sought to subjugate the local populations to their rule.

■ **1497-1499** Traveling around the Cape of Good Hope at the Southern tip of Africa, Portuguese explorer Vasco da Gama discovered a sea route from Europe to India.

■ **1510** The Portuguese military commander Alonso d'Albuquerque captured Goa, Calicut, and Melaka.

■ **1513** Ponce de León explored Florida. He also went in search of the legendary Fountain of Youth but — not surprisingly, since it is unlikely to exist — failed to locate it.

■ **1519-21** Hernando Cortés, a Spanish conquistador, explored and destroyed the civilization of the Aztecs of Mexico.

IN THE EARLY 1500S, PORTUGUESE SHIPS REGULARLY MADE CONQUESTS AT SEA.

■ **1532-35** The Spanish conquistador Francisco Pizarro destroyed the empire of the Incas in Peru.

■ **1535** The French navigator and explorer Jacques Cartier traveled up the St. Lawrence River to where Montreal, Canada, now stands.

■ **1577-80** Sir Francis Drake, knighted by Queen Elizabeth I, was the first Englishman to sail around the world. His forces defeated the Spanish Armada in 1588.

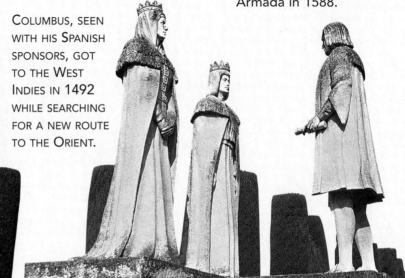

COLUMBUS, SEEN WITH HIS SPANISH SPONSORS, GOT TO THE WEST INDIES IN 1492 WHILE SEARCHING FOR A NEW ROUTE TO THE ORIENT.

- At Cebu, the oldest city in the Philippines, there are monuments commemorating both Magellan and Lapu-Lapu, the man who killed Magellan.

This portrait of Magellan (*left*) was painted especially for this book.

- A spacecraft named after Magellan was launched on May 4, 1989, and it began orbiting the planet Venus on August 10, 1990. Of all the planets in our solar system, Venus is the one most like Earth.

- A presidential rail car named after Ferdinand Magellan was presented to President Franklin D. Roosevelt in 1942. It is the only passenger rail car ever designated as a National Historic Landmark by the Government of the United States. Roosevelt traveled over fifty thousand miles in it during the course of his presidency.

- There is a statue of Magellan at Plaza Munoz Gamero, in Puerto Arenas, Chile.

- A postage stamp featuring a portrait of Ferdinand Magellan was issued in the Philippines in 1906.

- The Church of Basilica Minore del Santo Niño, the oldest church in the Philippines, has an image of the Holy Child given by Magellan to a rajah's wife. The so-called Magellan's Cross marks the spot where this rajah and his followers were baptized into the Christian religion in 1521.

- Several travel companies worldwide have used "Magellan" as a trade name. There is also a sailing center in Dallas, Texas, with his name.

- Two birds — the Magellan goose and the Magellan gull — both native to the Falkland Islands off South America, have been named after the explorer.

- In 1960, the USS *Triton* — the U.S. Navy's largest submarine — circumnavigated the globe, following Magellan's route but traveling underwater. The voyage took two months.

OVER THE YEARS

Listed (*left*) are a number of ways in which the memory of Ferdinand Magellan has been honored. The two remarkable feats for which he is most remembered are his personal circumnavigation of the world (although not made in one voyage) and his navigation in thirty-eight days of the strait now bearing his name. Considering how many of the strait's channels had to be investigated, Magellan's exploration was achieved with extraordinary speed.

GLOSSARY

anathema: something or someone hated.

apprentice: a young person who learns a trade through practical experience.

archipelago: a group of islands.

astrolabe: an early navigational instrument used to determine the position of celestial bodies such as stars.

astrologers: people who try to foretell the future from the positions of the stars and planets.

auction: the selling of goods to the highest bidders.

auxiliary: helping.

baptism: a ritual in which a person becomes a Christian after immersion in or sprinkling on of water.

camouflaged: blended into the colors of the environment as a form of hiding.

cannibal: a human who eats human flesh.

careening: turning over a ship to clean and seal its underside.

caulker: one who works to stop leaks on a ship.

chronicler: a person who keeps a continuous record of events; a diarist.

chronometer: a tool for measuring time.

circuit: a circular route.

circumnavigate: to sail completely around.

cloves: the dried buds of a tropical tree of the myrtle family that are used as an aromatic spice.

commodity: a useful or valuable economic good that can be traded.

concentric: having a shared center.

conquistador: a Spanish conqueror, especially a leader in the Spanish conquest of parts of Central and South America in the sixteenth century.

constellation: a group of stars.

court martial: a military court.

curriculum: the subjects taught in a school.

diplomacy: skill in handling relations between people and groups without causing hostility; tact.

Doldrums: the regions of the ocean near the equator where there are few winds.

Drake, Sir Francis: a sixteenth-century British admiral and explorer who served under Queen Elizabeth I.

epitaph: a brief description or saying on the tomb or grave of someone who is deceased.

equator: an imaginary line running horizontally around the center of the Earth that divides it into the northern and southern hemispheres.

flagship: the ship that carries the commander of a fleet.

flotilla: a fleet of ships.

footnote: additional information at the bottom of a page.

fresco: a wall-painting made using water-based pigments on freshly spread lime plaster.

galaxy: any of the large groups of stars and other matter found throughout the Universe.

grandee: a high-ranking nobleman, usually Spanish.

gruel: a thin porridge.

heathens: people who do not acknowledge the God of the Bible.

hemisphere: half of the globe divided through the center, either across at the equator (to make northern and southern hemispheres) or downward (to make eastern and western hemispheres).

high mass: a Christian tribute to God marked by the singing of special parts by the participants.

hold: a storeroom on a ship.

Holy Roman Emperor: the leader of a former confederation of German and Italian territories.

horizon: an imaginary line in the distance at the point where the sky and the Earth appear to meet.

horse latitudes: latitudes near 30 degrees north or south, where there are variable winds and calms.

hourglass: a device for measuring time in which a material (usually sand) runs from an upper part into a lower part in one hour.

junks: Chinese ships.

latitude: distance north or south of the equator, measured in degrees.

league: a unit of distance measuring about three miles.

longitude: distance east or west of an imaginary vertical line, such as that passing through Greenwich, London, England, and measured in degrees.

massacre: the slaughter of many usually unresisting humans.

Milky Way: the galaxy of which Earth's solar system is a part.

monsoon: 1) a seasonal wind in southern Asia; 2) the name given to the season characterized by this wind and heavy rainfall.

Muslims: people who follow the teachings of Muhammad and the religion of Islam.

mutiny: an uprising against the authority aboard a ship.

nautical: concerning ships or the sea.

pilot: the person in charge of steering a vessel.

Pole Star: the North Star, used by navigators as a guide.

pope: the head of the Roman Catholic Church.

promontory: a high rock projecting into the sea.

rajah: an Indian or Malay prince or chief.

stern: the back of a ship.

stick insect: a type of insect looking like a leaf or twig.

supernumerary: a member of a group beyond what is usual or necessary to the organization.

FOR FURTHER STUDY

BOOKS

Around the World in a Hundred Years: From Henry the Navigator to Magellan. Jean Fritz (Putnam Publishing Group)

Ferdinand Magellan and the Discovery of the World Ocean. Rebecca Stefoff (Chelsea House Publishers)

Ferdinand Magellan: First Explorer around the World. Arlene Bourgeois Molzahn (Enslow Publishers, Incorporated)

Ferdinand Magellan: First to Sail around the World. Milton Meltzer, Patricia Calvert, Harold Faber (Marshall Cavendish, Inc.)

Ferdinand Magellan: The First Voyage Around the World. Betty Burnett (Rosen Publishing Group, Incorporated)

Magellan and the First Voyage Around the World. Nancy Smiler Levinson (Houghton Mifflin Company)

To the Edge of the World. Michele Torrey (Alfred A. Knopf)

Travels of Ferdinand Magellan. Joanne Mattern (Raintree Publishers)

VIDEOS AND CD-ROMs

Explorers of the New World. (CD-ROM) (Library Video)

Ferdinand Magellan. Explorers of the World. (Schlessinger Media)

WEB SITES

Ferdinand Magellan.
www.mariner.org/age/magellan.html

Ferdinand Magellan: Circumnavigating the Globe.
www.ucalgary.ca/applied_history/tutor/ eurvoy/magellan.html

Ferdinand Magellan: The first to sail around the world.
www.nmm.ac.uk/site/request/setTemplate: singlecontent/contentTypeA/conWebDoc/ contentld/142

Fun Trivia: Magellan and his historic voyage!
www.funtrivia.com/ quizlistgold.cfm?cat=8620